大运中文
100 句

100 Chinese Sentences for the Chengdu 2021 FISU World University Games

中外语言交流合作中心　组编

Compiled by the Center for Language Education and Cooperation

组委会（以姓氏笔画为序）

沈　鹏　邵亦鹏　金瑞峰

秦　莉　黄立新　瞿嵩明

编委会

主　　编　　骆鹤凌　冉毅嵩
编　　者　　冯舒怡　周蕙杨　胡　琳
　　　　　　张末雨　马小飞　田海鲧
英文翻译　　Arthur Cheng（美）

支持单位

成都第 31 届世界大学生夏季运动会执委会
成都市教育局
成都市语言文字工作委员会办公室
四川出版发展公益基金会
四川新华乐知文化科技有限公司

Organizing Committee (in the order of the number of strokes in the members' surnames)

Shen Peng, Shao Yipeng, Jin Ruifeng,

Qin Li, Huang Lixin, Qu Songming

Editorial Board

Chief Editors	Luo Heling, Ran Yisong
Authors	Feng Shuyi, Zhou Huiyang, Hu Lin, Zhang Weiyu, Ma Xiaofei, Tian Haisu
English Translator	Arthur Cheng (U.S.)

Institutional Supporters

Executive Committee of the Chengdu 2021 FISU World University Games

Chengdu Municipal Education Bureau

Office of the Chengdu Municipal Language Commission

Sichuan Publishing Development Foundation

Xinhua Lucky Culture Technology Co., Ltd.

前言

第 31 届世界大学生夏季运动会即将于 2023 年 7 月 28 日至 8 月 8 日在中国成都举办。成都大运会是继 2001 年北京大运会、2011 年深圳大运会之后,中国第 3 次举办世界大学生夏季运动会。

本届成都大运会口号是"成都成就梦想"。"绿色、智慧、活力、共享"是成都大运会的办赛理念,"健康生活、积极运动"是成都大运会的主旨,诠释着体育精神和城市精神的融合。"带着你的梦到这里来,未来更美因为都有爱",正如成都大运会推广曲所唱,热情的成都向全球青年发出邀请,向全世界展现青年一代友好、团结、奋进的精神与活力,也向全世界传递中国的美好祝愿。大运会是体育竞技的大舞台,也是国际文化交流的大平台。来自世界各地的青年学生运动员和体育爱好者,将带着各自的文化、价值观和体育精神欢聚一堂,展现热情、活力、时尚的多彩生活与斑斓青春。

语言文字对于促进不同国家间相互理解、不同文明间交流互鉴具有十分重要的引领和支撑作用。学习不同语言能帮助我们了解不同国家人民的习俗、礼仪,促进交流与理解,学会包容和友善相处。《大运中文 100 句》是中外语言交流合作中心组织编写的语言服务手册。它遵循《国际中文教育中文水平等级标准》的要求,旨在通过展示 100 个中文常用句的基本含义和交际场景,满足大运会期间各国代表团在成都参赛和生活的基本需求,并通过介绍有代表性的大运会场馆、四川特色文化,传播大运精神,彰显人文风采,展现中国风貌。

热情的盛夏,多彩的青春,在这里,大运激情与美食、川剧、熊猫融合,成都以其独特的魅力和丰富的文化底蕴吸引世界的目光。相信成都大运会将为大家带来一场难忘的体育盛宴和文化体验。

中外语言交流合作中心

2023 年 6 月

Preface

The Chengdu 2021 FISU World University Games (hereafter Chengdu 2021 FISU Games) will be held in Chengdu, China, from July 28th to August 8th in 2023. Following Beijing in 2001 and Shenzhen in 2011, Chengdu is the third city on the Chinese mainland to host the summer Universiade.

The slogan of the Games is "Chengdu Makes Dreams Come True." Committed to the principle of hosting a "sustainable, smart, spirited, and sharing" Games, the event, with "promoting well-being through sporting activities" as its purpose, serves as a perfect combination of sportsmanship and the host city's values. "Bring your dreams here, for love makes a better future." As the promotional song sings, a vibrant Chengdu invites young people from all over the world to showcase their friendship, unity, enterprisingness, and vitality, and also takes this opportunity to convey China's good wishes to the world. The Games is not only a big arena for sports competitions but also a great platform for international cultural exchanges. Student-athletes and sports enthusiasts from across the globe will come together with their own cultures, values, and sporting philosophies to show their colorful lives and youthful vigor.

Language plays an essential guiding and supporting role in promoting mutual understanding among countries as well as exchanges and mutual learning among civilizations. Learning different languages can help gain familiarity with customs and etiquette of different nations, promote communication and understanding, and boost inclusiveness and friendliness. The book *100 Chinese Sentences for the Chengdu 2021 FISU World University Games* is a language service manual compiled by the Center for Language Education and Cooperation. Following the Chinese Proficiency Grading Standards for International Chinese Language Education, it aims to meet the basic needs of foreign delegations during the Games in Chengdu by showing the meanings of 100 commonly used Chinese sentences and the scenarios where they are used. Representative Games venues and Sichuan's distinctive cultures are also featured in a bid to spread the Games spirit, demonstrate cultural glamour, and offer insights into contemporary China.

In this passionate summer, young athletes from across the world, blending with local gourmet food, Sichuan opera, and giant pandas, will bring Chengdu, a uniquely charming city rich in cultural deposits, into the spotlight of the world. We believe that the Chengdu 2021 FISU Games will bring everyone unforgettable sports memories and cultural experiences.

Center for Language Education and Cooperation
June 2023

成都第 31 届世界大学生夏季运动会会徽
Chengdu 2021 FISU Games Emblem

成都大运会会徽主体以世界大学生运动会英文（Universiade）首字母"U"为基础形态，通过曲线切割的方式将"U"分割成朱红、明黄、翠绿、湖蓝四个渐变色块，对应成都大运会"绿色、智慧、活力、共享"的办赛理念，并与国际大体联标志元素一脉相承。

会徽在基础形态上还糅合了"太阳神鸟"与"凤凰"这两种典型的中国元素,象征古蜀文明与天府文化的古今交融,"凤首"与"凤尾"的抽象设计勾勒出一只灵动的瑞鸟,表达人们对光明的渴望和追逐梦想的决心,彰显自强不息、昂扬向上的精神面貌。

Similar in shape to the letter "U" from the English word "Universiade," the main body of the emblem is composed of four gradient color blocks of rich red, bright yellow, jade green, and lake blue which represent the four components of the guiding principle of hosting a "sustainable, smart, spirited, and sharing" Games, and is also in harmony with the FISU logo.

The basic design combines two typical Chinese elements, the Golden Sun Bird and the phoenix, symbolizing the integration of ancient Shu civilization and modern Tianfu culture. The abstract designs of the bird's head and tail are meant to represent its agility and auspiciousness, conveying people's desire for brightness and determination to pursue dreams, and highlighting a spirit of constant self-improvement and an enterprising attitude.

▶ 成都第31届世界大学生夏季运动会口号
Chengdu 2021 FISU Games Slogan

成都成就梦想

Chengdu Makes Dreams Come True

成都成就梦想

Chengdu Makes Dreams Come True

  成都大运会口号为"成都成就梦想",寓意全球大学生运动员以梦想之名相约成都,书写青春风华,成就明日之星。

  大学生作为整个社会力量中最积极、最有生气的力量,是时代的"追梦人"。每个大学生心中都有一个梦想,世界大学生运动会是全球大学生同场竞技和交流的盛会,也是汇聚青春梦想的舞台。成都大运会将见证全球大学生运动员挥洒汗水、挑战极限、实现梦想的精彩过程。

The slogan, "Chengdu Makes Dreams Come True," implies that college student-athletes from all over the world gather together in Chengdu to pursue their dreams to compose a new chapter of their youthful splendor and to strive to become the stars of tomorrow.

As the most active and energetic element among all forces in society, college students are all contemporary dream chasers since each and every one of them has a dream. The Chengdu 2021 FISU Games, an arena for competition and exchange and also a stage where youthful dreams mingle and shine, will witness young people from all over the world sweat and strive as they challenge their limits and realize their dreams.

目录
Contents

01 见面 ········· *01*
Greetings

02 告别 ········· *07*
Farewell

03 感谢 ········· *13*
Expressing Gratitude

04 道歉 ········· *19*
Apologies

05 喜好 ········· *25*
Expressing Preferences

06 注册 ········· *31*
Accreditation

07 交友 ········· *37*
Making Friends

08 问询 ········· *45*
Inquiries

09 比赛 ········· *51*
Sports Competitions

10 夸奖 ········· *57*
Responding to Compliments

11	活动 · · · · · 63 Event Participation	16	游览 · · · · · 103 Touring
12	设施 · · · · · 69 Facilities	17	购物 · · · · · 113 Shopping
13	交通 · · · · · 75 Transportation	18	邀请 · · · · · 121 Invitations
14	饮食 · · · · · 83 Dining	19	聚会 · · · · · 127 Participating in Gatherings
15	住宿 · · · · · 93 Accommodations	20	祝福 · · · · · 133 Expressing Good Wishes

01 / 见面
Greetings

基本句 | Basic Sentences

1 你好!
Hello!

2 早上好!
Good morning!

3 我叫赵蓉,是中国人。
My name is Zhao Rong and I'm Chinese.

4 很高兴认识你。
It's a pleasure to meet you.

5 欢迎来到成都。
Welcome to Chengdu.

词汇拓展 | Vocabulary Extension

shàng wǔ
上 午
morning

xià wǔ
下 午
afternoon

wǎn shang
晚 上
evening

zuó tiān
昨 天
yesterday

jīn tiān
今 天
today

míng tiān
明 天
tomorrow

中文常用称谓
Common Ways to Address People in Chinese

中文里的称谓丰富多彩,在社会交往中,如何称呼对方直接体现出双方之间的亲疏、了解程度、尊重与否以及个人修养等。一个得体的称呼,会令彼此如沐春风,为往后的交往打下良好的基础。

· **泛尊称**

可直接称呼女士、先生。

· **行业性称呼**

可在职业前加姓氏,如王教练、李老师、张医生。

· **对朋友、熟人的称呼**

可直称姓名,如李华、张晓丽。

There are many ways to address people in Chinese. In social situations, how to address someone is related to the closeness, mutual understanding, and mutual respect between the two sides, as well as personal qualities. Using a proper way to address someone helps foster a comfortable ambience for both sides and lay solid groundwork for future interactions.

• **To show respect**
Address the person as *nüshi* (Ms.) or *xiansheng* (Mr.).

• **Based on professions**
Add the person's family name (or full name) in front of their profession or position, i.e. Wang jiaolian (Coach Wang), Li laoshi (Teacher Li), and Zhang yisheng (Doctor Zhang).

• **For friends and close associates**
Address the person by their full name, i.e. Li Hua or Zhang Xiaoli.

02 / 告别
Farewell

基本句 | Basic Sentences

6 再(zài)见(jiàn)!
Goodbye!

7 明(míng)天(tiān)见(jiàn)!
See you tomorrow!

8 慢(màn)走(zǒu)!
Goodbye! Take care!

9 下(xià)次(cì)再(zài)会(huì)!
Look forward to seeing you again!

10 这(zhè)是(shì)我(wǒ)的(de)电(diàn)话(huà),以(yǐ)后(hòu)常(cháng)联(lián)系(xì)。
This is my phone number. Let's keep in touch.

词汇拓展 | Vocabulary Extension

1	2	3	4	5
yī	èr	sān	sì	wǔ
一	二	三	四	五
one	two	three	four	five

6	7	8	9	10
liù	qī	bā	jiǔ	shí
六	七	八	九	十
six	seven	eight	nine	ten

中文常用告别语
Common Ways to Bid Farewell in Chinese

告别语作为日常交往结束的标志,是社交生活中必不可少的部分。中文的告别语尤其注重相互关切和敬重他人的礼貌原则。

·用对双方相处的评价作为告别语

例如,"今天的交谈很有收获,谢谢你"。

·用表达关切与祝愿作为告别语

例如,"慢走""多保重""一路顺风"。

·用表达再次相会愿望作为告别语

例如,"期待再次见面""以后有空多聚聚"。

Farewell signals the conclusion of a daily interaction, and it is an unavoidable part of socializing. In Chinese, the etiquette principle of showing care and respect for others is particularly emphasized when bidding farewell.

• **To comment on the interaction between the two sides**
For example, "I learned a lot from our talk today, thank you."

• **To extend care and good wishes**
For example, "Take care." "Take good care of yourself." "Wish you a safe trip."

• **To express the wish to meet again**
For example, "Looking forward to the next meeting." "Let's meet more often in the future."

03 / 感谢
Expressing Gratitude

基本句 | Basic Sentences

11 谢谢!
Thank you!

12 非常感谢!
Thanks so much!

13 请在前面路边停车,麻烦你了。
Please park on the side of the road ahead, thank you.

14 不客气!
You're welcome!

15 有你的帮助,真是太好了。
It's great to have your help.

词汇拓展 | Vocabulary Extension

qián	hòu	zuǒ	yòu
前	后	左	右
front	back	left	right

dōng	nán	xī	běi
东	南	西	北
east	south	west	north

中文常用感谢语
Common Ways to Express Gratitude in Chinese

感谢是世界各国文化所共有的一种礼貌行为,是对他人帮助的认可与赞赏。除直接感谢语外,中文里的间接感谢语以其特别的语言形式和丰富的词汇组合更凸显了中国文化的博大精深。

· **直接感谢语**

例如,"多谢""谢谢""非常感谢"。

· **间接感谢语**

例如,"以后你有什么事,尽管开口""让你费心了""给你添麻烦了""我们是老朋友了,别这么客气"。

Showing appreciation is a polite behavior that exists in all cultures, and it is a way to show approval and praise to someone who has helped. Apart from saying "thank you" directly, the Chinese people use indirect expressions and a diverse combination of terms to show gratitude in ways that embody the profundity of Chinese culture.

• **Direct ways to show appreciation**
For example, "Thanks." "Thank you." "Thank you very much."

• **Indirect ways to show appreciation**
For example, "If you need any help in the future, just let me know." "Thanks for going through all the troubles." "Sorry for all the inconvenience." "You didn't have to do that. We are buddies."

04 / 道歉
Apologies

基本句 | Basic Sentences

16 对不起。
duì bu qǐ
I'm sorry.

17 抱歉，我听不懂。
bào qiàn, wǒ tīng bu dǒng
Sorry, I don't understand.

18 不好意思，耽误你的时间了。
bù hǎo yì si, dān wu nǐ de shí jiān le
Sorry for taking so much of your time.

19 打扰你了，请见谅。
dǎ rǎo nǐ le, qǐng jiàn liàng
Sorry for troubling you.

20 没关系。
méi guān xi
It's all right.

词汇拓展 | Vocabulary Extension

2023 / 07 / 28

nián
年
year

yuè
月
month

rì
日
day

19 : 59 : 50

shí
时
hour

fēn
分
minute

miǎo
秒
second

jiǔ diǎn
九 点
nine o'clock

jiǔ diǎn yí kè
九 点 一 刻
a quarter past nine

jiǔ diǎn bàn
九 点 半
half past nine

中文常用致歉语
Common Ways to Apologize in Chinese

致歉语是礼貌用语的重要组成部分。在人际交往中由于自己的问题,给别人带来不快、损失甚至伤害的时候,我们可以通过致歉语向对方表达歉意,以维护良好的人际关系。

· **直接道歉,明确表示歉意**

例如,"对不起""很抱歉""请你原谅"。

· **承担责任,承认错误**

例如,"这件事是我的责任,请你谅解""都是因为我没有经验,对不起"。

· **程度较轻的客气表达**

例如,"不好意思,请你让一下"。

Apology is an important component of courteous interaction. During interpersonal communication, when you caused unhappiness, loss or even injury to others, we can make an apology in order to maintain sound interpersonal relationships.

- **Apologize directly and clearly**

For example, "Sorry." "Really sorry." "Please forgive me."

- **Take responsibility and admit wrongdoing**

For example, "It's my fault, please forgive me." "It's because I'm inexperienced. I'm sorry."

- **Use moderately courteous expressions**

For example, "Excuse me, could you move a little?"

05 / 喜好
Expressing Preferences

基本句 | Basic Sentences

21 wǒ hěn xǐ huan
我很喜欢。
I really like it.

22 zhè ge zěn me yàng
这个怎么样?
How about this one?

23 nǐ jué de nǎ yí gè zuì hǎo kàn
你觉得哪一个最好看?
Which one do you think looks the best?

24 wǒ gèng xǐ huan hóng sè de, bái sè bú tài shì hé wǒ
我更喜欢红色的,白色不太适合我。
I prefer the red one, because the white one doesn't really suit me.

25 zhè shì wǒ dì yī cì lái chéng dū, wǒ hěn kāi xīn
这是我第一次来成都,我很开心。
This is my first time in Chengdu and I'm having a great time.

词汇拓展 | Vocabulary Extension

hóng sè **红色** red	huáng sè **黄色** yellow
lǜ sè **绿色** green	lán sè **蓝色** blue
bái sè **白色** white	hēi sè **黑色** black
shēn sè **深色** dark color	qiǎn sè **浅色** light color

中文常用委婉语
Common Euphemisms in Chinese

中文委婉语是对不能、不便、不愿直接说明的事情采用令人愉快的、委婉有礼的说法,体现出中国的文化特性、思维方法及行为方式。

·自谦的表达

例如,面对他人的赞美和夸奖,中国人常说"过奖了""哪里哪里"。

·对人尊敬的表达

例如,与长辈交谈,自称"晚辈";询问他人姓名,使用敬语"您贵姓"。

·委婉有礼的表达

例如,若想表达"菜咸了",可以委婉地说"菜很好吃,如果再少放一点儿盐就更美味了"。

Mild or indirect expressions are usually used when you can't, are inconvenient to or unwilling to say something bad or unpleasant directly. This category of expressions embodies the cultural characteristics, mindset, and behavior of the Chinese people.

• **To show modesty**
For example, when being praised or commended, a Chinese would often reply with "you flatter me" or "I am flattered."

• **To show respect**
For example, when speaking with the elders, address oneself as "junior" or "younger generation." When asking for someone's name, it is polite to use honorific language and ask, "May I ask your distinguished surname?"

• **Be indirect and polite when stating an opinion**
For example, if a dish is too salty, indirectly say so with something like "that's tasty, but it'd be better with a little less salt."

06 / 注册
Accreditation

基本句 | Basic Sentences

26 qǐng wèn zài nǎ lǐ zhù cè
请问在哪里注册?
Excuse me, where do I go for accreditation?

27 zhǔ xìn xī zhōng xīn zài yī céng
主信息中心在一层。
The Main Information Center is on the first floor.

28 wǒ bù zhī dào zěn me yù yuē
我不知道怎么预约。
I don't know how to book an appointment.

29 qǐng zài shuō yí biàn
请再说一遍。
I beg your pardon.

30 hái yǒu qí tā shǒu xù yào bàn lǐ ma
还有其他手续要办理吗?
Is there anything else I need to do?

词汇拓展 | Vocabulary Extension

hù zhào
护 照
passport

shǒu jī
手 机
mobile phone

xíng li
行 李
luggage

fáng kǎ
房 卡
room card

shēn fèn zhù cè kǎ
身 份 注 册 卡
accreditation card

zhǔ xìn xī zhōng xīn
主 信 息 中 心
Main Information Center

zhǔ zhù cè zhōng xīn
主 注 册 中 心
Main Accreditation Center

sài shì xìn xī zhōng xīn
赛 事 信 息 中 心
Sports Information Center

成都第31届世界大学生夏季运动会运动员村
Chengdu 2021 FISU Games Athletes' Village

成都大运村位于成都大学校园内,整体占地面积约80万平方米,距市中心仅12千米。大运村秉承"开放、融合、绿色、智慧"的规划设计理念,为来蓉参赛代表团提供住宿、餐饮、健身、商业、休闲娱乐、文化交流等多种服务,通过提供安全舒适的生活和工作环境,保障运动员以最佳状态参赛。同时,村内还会举行不同主题、多种形式的文化活动,突出中国元素、四川特征和天府文化,展现青春风采,营造浓厚的大运会文化氛围,丰富运动员的赛后生活。大运会结束后,大运村将用于校园教学,继续发挥其功能。

The village, located within the campus of Chengdu University, covers an overall area of approximately 800,000 square meters and is only 12 kilometers away from the city center. Committed to the principle of being "open, integrated, green, and intelligent," it provides its residents with various services such as accommodations, catering, fitness, business, leisure and entertainment, and cultural exchange. The safe, comfortable living and working environment ensures that athletes compete in their best form. Moreover, multiple cultural events of different themes and forms are to be held with Chinese elements, Sichuan features, and Tianfu culture highlighted, in a bid to showcase youthful vitality, foster a strong Games atmosphere, and enrich athletes' post-Games life. After the Games end, it will be used as a site for on-campus teaching.

07 / 交友
Making Friends

基本句 | Basic Sentences

31 你在哪个城市上大学？
Where do you go to school?

32 毕业后你想从事什么工作？
What's your plan after graduation?

33 我现在读大学二年级。
I am now into my second year in university.

34 明天比赛加油！
Good luck at the Games tomorrow!

35 我们一起去看开幕式吧。
Let's watch the Opening Ceremony together.

词汇拓展 | Vocabulary Extension

běn kē shēng
本科生
undergraduate student

shuò shì yán jiū shēng
硕士研究生
master's student

bó shì yán jiū shēng
博士研究生
doctoral student

dài biǎo tuán
代表团
delegation

zhì yuàn zhě
志愿者
volunteer

jì zhě
记者
journalist

成都东安湖体育公园(世界大运公园)
Chengdu Dong'an Lake Sports Park (World University Games Park)

  成都东安湖体育公园包含"一场三馆"。"一场"为4万座位的大运会主体育场,用于举办大运会开幕式;"三馆"为1.8万座位的多功能体育馆(体操项目比赛场馆)、3000座位的游泳跳水馆(游泳项目比赛场馆)和小球馆(体操项目训练馆),还包括大运会火炬塔、桃源驿、银沙驿等景观设施。

大运会主体育场呈圆形设计，体育场的穹顶是一个极具科技感和未来感的"飞碟"造型，表面绘有代表悠久古蜀文化精髓的太阳神鸟图案。"三馆"采用由银色铝制元素构成的百叶幕墙，这些百叶朝中心方向逐渐翻转打开，展现出内部不同功能空间的形态及颜色。每座建筑都有自己的颜色代码，便于访客在场地及体育馆内辨认方位。三座体育馆在平面上呈正方形，由一个共同的基座相连。

The Dong'an Lake Sports Park boasts one stadium and three gymnasiums. The former refers to the main stadium of the Chengdu 2021 FISU Games, which has 40,000 seats and will be the venue for the Opening Ceremony. The latter include a 18,000-seat multi-purpose gymnasium for gymnastics competitions, a 3,000-seat natatorium for swimming competitions, and a small gymnasium for gymnastics practices. There are also the Chengdu 2021 FISU Games Torch Tower, Taoyuanyi, Yinshayi, and other landscape facilities in the Park.

The main stadium has a circular form, with a highly futuristic flying saucer-shaped dome featuring an artistic expression of the Golden Sun Bird as the embodiment of the ancient Shu culture. The three gymnasiums are equipped with aluminum louver curtain walls, and when the silver-colored louver panels rotate inwards, the forms and colors of the different functional spaces inside are revealed. Each structure has its own color coding system to help visitors identify where they are. The three buildings are square in shape, and are connected by a single base.

08 / 问询
Inquiries

基本句 | Basic Sentences

36 我需要帮助。
wǒ xū yào bāng zhù
I need help.

37 我不太舒服，你能带我去看医生吗?
wǒ bú tài shū fu, nǐ néng dài wǒ qù kàn yī shēng ma
I don't feel well, could you take me to the doctor?

38 对不起，我现在有急事。
duì bu qǐ, wǒ xiàn zài yǒu jí shì
Sorry, I need to deal with something urgent right now.

39 快走，我们要迟到了。
kuài zǒu, wǒ men yào chí dào le
Hurry up! We're going to be late.

40 我的手机快没电了，请问哪里可以充电?
wǒ de shǒu jī kuài méi diàn le, qǐng wèn nǎ lǐ kě yǐ chōng diàn
Where can I charge my phone? Battery is about to run out.

词汇拓展 | Vocabulary Extension

tóu	shǒu
头	手
head	hand

tuǐ	jiǎo
腿	脚
leg	foot

téng	yūn
疼	晕
ache	dizzy

gǎn mào	ké sou
感冒	咳嗽
cold	cough

成都凤凰山体育公园
Chengdu Fenghuangshan Sports Park

成都凤凰山体育公园包含"一场一馆","一场"指的是按照FIFA标准建设的专业足球场,配备锚固草系统,能同时容纳6万名观众;"一馆"指的是共1.8万座位的综合体育馆,为成都大运会篮球项目比赛场馆。综合体育馆可实现场馆快速转换,当铺上可拆装的体育运动专用木地板后,场馆就变身为可举办国际篮球比赛的专业篮球馆;当拆下时,就可以变成冰球场,场地转换仅需4个小时,完全满足各项顶级赛事对场地硬件的要求。

The Fenghuangshan Sports Park consists of one stadium and one gymnasium, namely a FIFA-standard football stadium equipped with a hybrid grass pitch and enough seating for 60,000 spectators, and a multi-purpose gymnasium with 18,000 seats that will function as the basketball competition venue of the Chengdu 2021 FISU Games. The latter is outfitted with removable flooring designed for sports. When the flooring is installed, the gymnasium turns into a venue for professional basketball competitions, and with the flooring removed, it transforms into an ice hockey rink. The installation or removal of flooring can be completed in four hours, with hardware requirements for various top-level competitions fully satisfied.

09 / 比赛
Sports Competitions

基本句 | Basic Sentences

41 今天的比赛太精彩了！
jīn tiān de bǐ sài tài jīng cǎi le
The game today was incredible!

42 我要感谢我的教练和队友。
wǒ yào gǎn xiè wǒ de jiào liàn hé duì yǒu
I have my coach and teammates to thank.

43 没关系，你们已经尽力了。
méi guān xi nǐ men yǐ jīng jìn lì le
It's all right. You've done your best.

44 他打破纪录了！
tā dǎ pò jì lù le
He set a new record!

45 祝贺你取得好成绩！
zhù hè nǐ qǔ dé hǎo chéng jì
Congratulations on your accomplishment!

词汇拓展 | Vocabulary Extension

yù sài
预赛
preliminary

bàn jué sài
半决赛
semi-final

jué sài
决赛
final

gè rén sài
个人赛
individual competition

shuāng rén sài
双人赛
doubles/pairs competition

tuán tǐ sài
团体赛
team competition

成都第 31 届世界大学生夏季运动会吉祥物
Chengdu 2021 FISU Games Official Mascot

成都大运会吉祥物是一只名为"蓉宝"的大熊猫。蓉宝手持"31"字样的大运火炬，呈奔跑姿态；耳朵、眼睛、尾巴为火焰造型，传递着成都的热情；面部构思参考传统艺术瑰宝——川剧的脸谱样式，是川剧这一中国非物质文化遗产与时俱进的创新体现。

The official mascot is a giant panda named Rongbao. It is running while holding the Chengdu 2021 FISU Games torch which bears the number 31. Its ears, eyes, and tail are shaped as flames, conveying the passion and hospitality of the host city. The facial design draws inspiration from a cherished traditional art form, the facial makeup of Sichuan opera, manifesting the continued innovation of the opera as an intangible cultural heritage element in China.

10 / 夸奖

Responding to Compliments

基本句 | Basic Sentences

46 xiè xie nǐ de gǔ lì
谢谢你的鼓励。
Thanks for your encouragement.

47 nǐ guò jiǎng le
你过奖了。
I am flattered.

48 wǒ huì jì xù nǔ lì de
我会继续努力的。
I will keep trying.

49 zhè shì dà jiā de gōng láo
这是大家的功劳。
Credit goes to everyone.

50 nǐ yě zuò de hěn hǎo, wǒ yào xiàng nǐ xué xí
你也做得很好,我要向你学习。
You've done well too. I should learn from you.

词汇拓展 | Vocabulary Extension

guàn jūn
冠军
champion

jīn pái
金牌
gold medal

yà jūn
亚军
first runner-up

yín pái
银牌
silver medal

jì jūn
季军
second runner-up

tóng pái
铜牌
bronze medal

成都第31届世界大学生夏季运动会奖牌
Chengdu 2021 FISU Games Medals

成都大运会奖牌"蓉光"取自成都的简称"蓉",同时寓有"荣光"之意。奖牌创意以"五洲融合、天府文化、赛事标识系统、成都成就梦想"为核心。

奖牌"蓉光"之上镌刻着良渚玉鸟、太阳神鸟、商周铜人形器、战国青铜矛、汉代"五星出东方利中国"织锦和汉代五铢钱等图画元素,以及一段关于汉字演变史的文字,彰显璀璨辉煌的中华文明和成都迎接大运盛事的从容与自信,同时蕴含对大运健儿成就梦想的美好期许。

The medals are named Rongguang, the character 蓉, *rong*, being an abbreviation of Chengdu and the character 光, *guang*, meaning glory. The design is centered on the following aspects: integration of the five continents, Tianfu culture, Chengdu 2021 FISU Games logo system, and the slogan "Chengdu Makes Dreams Come True."

They are engraved with pictorial elements deriving from the Liangzhu Jade Bird, the Golden Sun Bird, bronze figures of the Shang and Zhou dynasties, bronze spears of the Warring States period, the brocade piece with woven characters meaning "five stars rise in the east, benefiting China," and Wuzhu coin of the Han dynasty, along with a text about the evolution of Chinese written characters. All these elements highlight the splendid Chinese civilization, the confidence of Chengdu to host a successful Games, and good wishes to the athletes for achieving their dreams.

11 / 活动
Event Participation

基本句 | Basic Sentences

51 <ruby>请<rt>qǐng</rt></ruby> <ruby>问<rt>wèn</rt></ruby> <ruby>商<rt>shāng</rt></ruby> <ruby>业<rt>yè</rt></ruby> <ruby>中<rt>zhōng</rt></ruby> <ruby>心<rt>xīn</rt></ruby> <ruby>在<rt>zài</rt></ruby> <ruby>哪<rt>nǎ</rt></ruby> <ruby>里<rt>lǐ</rt></ruby>？
Excuse me, where is the commercial center?

52 <ruby>她<rt>tā</rt></ruby> <ruby>准<rt>zhǔn</rt></ruby> <ruby>备<rt>bèi</rt></ruby> <ruby>去<rt>qù</rt></ruby> <ruby>体<rt>tǐ</rt></ruby> <ruby>验<rt>yàn</rt></ruby> <ruby>太<rt>tài</rt></ruby> <ruby>极<rt>jí</rt></ruby> <ruby>拳<rt>quán</rt></ruby>。
She is getting ready to go to the t'ai chi ch'uan event.

53 <ruby>这<rt>zhè</rt></ruby> <ruby>个<rt>ge</rt></ruby> <ruby>活<rt>huó</rt></ruby> <ruby>动<rt>dòng</rt></ruby> <ruby>真<rt>zhēn</rt></ruby> <ruby>有<rt>yǒu</rt></ruby> <ruby>意<rt>yì</rt></ruby> <ruby>思<rt>si</rt></ruby>！
This event is interesting!

54 <ruby>他<rt>tā</rt></ruby> <ruby>去<rt>qù</rt></ruby> <ruby>看<rt>kàn</rt></ruby> <ruby>艺<rt>yì</rt></ruby> <ruby>术<rt>shù</rt></ruby> <ruby>展<rt>zhǎn</rt></ruby> <ruby>览<rt>lǎn</rt></ruby> <ruby>了<rt>le</rt></ruby>。
He has gone to the art exhibition.

55 <ruby>我<rt>wǒ</rt></ruby> <ruby>可<rt>kě</rt></ruby> <ruby>以<rt>yǐ</rt></ruby> <ruby>和<rt>hé</rt></ruby> <ruby>你<rt>nǐ</rt></ruby> <ruby>交<rt>jiāo</rt></ruby> <ruby>换<rt>huàn</rt></ruby> <ruby>徽<rt>huī</rt></ruby> <ruby>章<rt>zhāng</rt></ruby> <ruby>吗<rt>ma</rt></ruby>？
Would you like to exchange badges?

词汇拓展 | Vocabulary Extension

shǔ xiù
蜀绣
Shu (Sichuan) embroidery

liǎn pǔ
脸谱
Chinese opera facial makeup

xiāng bāo
香包
sachet making

jiǎn zhǐ
剪纸
paper cutting

zhú biān
竹编
bamboo weaving

pí yǐng
皮影
shadow puppetry

shéng biān
绳编
string weaving

nián huà
年画
Chinese New Year painting

成都第31届世界大学生夏季运动会火炬
Chengdu 2021 FISU Games Torch

　　成都大运会火炬"蓉火"寓有"融合""包容"之意,其设计细节丰富。火炬正面以大熊猫为主元素,顶部是太阳神鸟,侧面犹似三星堆青铜立人造型;火炬上端开口的竹叶孔造型,既满足火焰的进气需求,又与火炬正面的大熊猫元素完美融合。火炬运用的整体色彩像彩虹一样多彩渐变,展现出大学生们的青春、活力和无限希望。

　　小小火炬,满满寓意,丰富的中华文化符号在创新工艺设计中焕发新生,使得"蓉火"优雅、时尚、内涵厚重。

The torch Ronghuo conveys the meaning of harmony and inclusiveness. Its front side features a giant panda, with its top incorporating the image of the Golden Sun Bird. On the side view, it looks like the standing bronze figure from Sanxingdui. The small openings on its upper part are cleverly carved into the shape of bamboo leaves, which not only provide air intake required by the flame, but also perfectly blend in with the giant panda element. The overall hue is as gorgeous and colorful as the rainbow, representing the infinite vigor and promise of college students.

The torch is small yet brimming with meanings. A host of symbols of Chinese culture are revitalized in the innovative design, making Ronghuo both stylishly elegant and culturally enriched.

12 / 设施
Facilities

基本句 | Basic Sentences

56 怎么上网?
How can I get online?

57 我们要去换人民币。
We need to exchange foreign currency for RMB.

58 前往闭幕式的班车几点出发?在哪里乘车?
When does the shuttle to the Closing Ceremony leave? Where is the shuttle?

59 我想理发。
I want to get a haircut.

60 我想办理国际货运,请问在哪里办?
Where can I get international freight service?

词汇拓展 | Vocabulary Extension

yín háng
银行
bank

yóu zhèng fú wù
邮政服务
postal service

yī liáo zhōng xīn
医疗中心
medical center

chāo shì
超市
supermarket

gān xǐ diàn
干洗店
dry cleaner's

xiān huā diàn
鲜花店
florist's

kā fēi tīng
咖啡厅
coffee shop

diàn yǐng yuàn
电影院
cinema

jiàn shēn zhōng xīn
健身中心
fitness center

成都露天音乐公园(闭幕式地点)
Chengdu Open-Air Music Park (site of the Closing Ceremony)

成都露天音乐公园是一座以音乐为主题,集文化演艺、休闲娱乐、旅游观光等功能于一体的大型城市公园。

成都露天音乐公园是国内顶级露天音乐演艺场地及国内唯一一座露天音乐主题园区。公园的整体景观设计融入了太阳神鸟文化、天府文化、凤凰文化、古蜀音乐文化,同时兼具国际化风格。其最大特色是建有目前世界最大的全景声半露天半室内双面剧场,剧场横向跨度180米、高50米,顶部可投影穹顶天幕面积约1万平方米,草坪观演区可容纳约4.7万名观众。

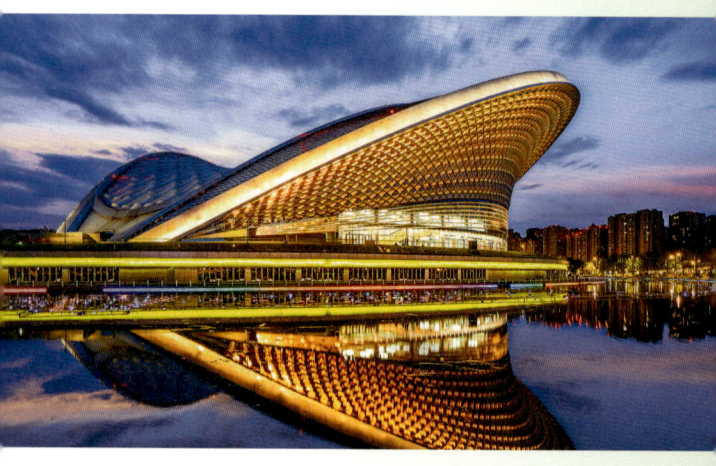

The Chengdu Open-Air Music Park is a large, music-themed urban park that incorporates functions such as cultural performance, leisure, recreation, tourism, and sightseeing.

The Chengdu Open-Air Music Park is one of China's top outdoor music performance venue and the country's one and only open-air music-themed park. The complex's overall design incorporates Golden Sun Bird culture, Tianfu culture, phoenix culture, and ancient Shu music culture, while also taking in international elements. The most unique highlight is a half-indoor, half-outdoor, double-sided Dolby Atmos theater that is currently the world's largest of its kind. The theater boasts a horizontal span of 180 meters, a height of 50 meters, a projection dome measuring roughly 10,000 square meters in area, and enough space in the lawn viewing area to accommodate approximately 47,000 spectators.

13 / 交通
Transportation

基本句 | Basic Sentences

61 到最近的地铁站，怎么走？
How do I get to the nearest metro station?

62 从这里到春熙路有几站？
How many stops are there from here to Chunxi Road?

63 请问这是到大运村的车吗？
Is this the shuttle to the FISU Games Village?

64 我用导航查看一下路线。
Let me check the route on the navigation app.

65 我想去锦里。
I want to go to Jinli Street.

成都方言 | Chengdu Dialect

den³ har¹
等 哈儿: 等一会儿
please wait a minute

gao³ bu² yin²
搞 不 赢: 来不及
there is no time

di³ nong³ dao³ guai³
抵 拢 倒 拐: 直走到底, 再转弯
go straight all the way, then make a turn

yao⁴ de²
要 得: 行, 可以
a response meaning "I agree" or "OK"

mo² de¹ si⁴
没 得 事: 没事儿
it's all right

hao³ ma³
好 嘛: 好吧
OK; fine

说明: 成都话的阴、阳、上、去四声, 用"1、2、3、4"表示, 标在音节右上角。

According to *The Dictionary of the Sichuan Dialect* published by Sichuan People's Publishing House in 2018, there are four tones in the Chengdu dialect, namely *yin* (阴), *yang* (阳), *shang* (上), and *qu* (去). In this book, they are indicated by the numerals 1, 2, 3, and 4 respectively which are written in superscript to the right of the syllables.

交通工具怎么选？
Which Mode of Transportation to Choose?

成都的城市交通已经在向智慧交通转型升级，并在探索着超大城市交通治理的新理念、新路径、新方式，在改善城市拥堵状况的同时，提升了居民的出行体验。

如果你想一边运动，一边欣赏成都公园城市的美景，你可以轻松扫描二维码，骑上共享单车，来一场说走就走的骑行；如果你追求绿色低碳，公交地铁就再适合不过了，扫码、投币、刷卡，总有适合你的支付方式；如果你想单独乘车，出租车或者网约车就非常适合你，随手一招或者网上输入你想去的地方，就有专车来接你。

成都，就是这么方便。

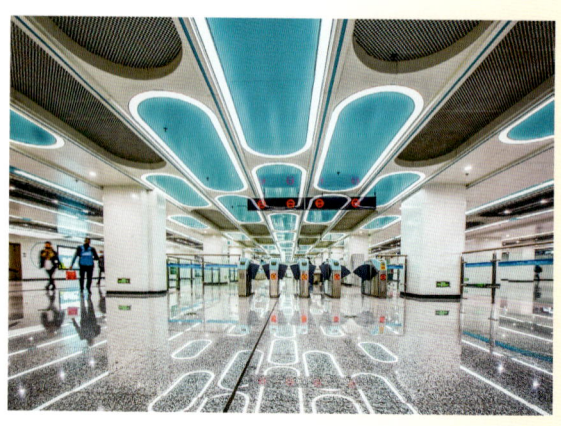

The urban transportation system in Chengdu has already been upgraded to a smarter one, and efforts are being made to explore new ideas, approaches, and methods for managing transportation in this megacity behemoth. All this contributes to the mitigation of traffic congestion and improvement of people's travel experience.

If you want to exercise and enjoy the beautiful scenery of the city at the same time, you can just scan a QR code for a spontaneous shared-bike ride. If you pursue green and low-carbon travel, public transportation such as buses and subways are the best choices. You can pay by scanning QR codes, inserting coins, or swiping credit/debit cards, and there is always a means that suits you. If you want to take a ride alone, taxis or ride-hailing services are very suitable for you. You can just wave your hand or input the destination online, and a tailored taxi will come to pick you up.

Travel in Chengdu is so convenient.

14 / 饮食
Dining

基本句 | Basic Sentences

66 wǒ chī sù
我 吃 素。
I am vegetarian.

67 wǒ men diǎn yí gè yuān yāng huǒ guō, yào wēi là
我 们 点 一 个 鸳 鸯 火 锅，要 微 辣。
We want a *yuanyang* (double-flavor) hot pot, with light spiciness for the red soup.

68 wèi dào hǎo jí le
味 道 好 极 了！
This tastes great!

69 wǒ chī bǎo le
我 吃 饱 了。
I am full.

70 zài lái yí fèn
再 来 一 份。
Another order, please.

成都方言 | Chengdu Dialect

ba¹ si²⁻⁴
巴 适：令人满意
gratifying

ngan¹ yi⁴
安 逸：舒服、舒适
comfortable; nice

nao³ banr⁴
老 板 儿：一种称呼，可指店主
a way to call people, which can refer to the owner of a shop

bin¹ qian⁴
冰 欠：很冰
icy cold

min¹ tian²
蜜 甜：很甜
very sweet

fei¹ na²
飞 辣：非常辣
very spicy

地道美食吃什么?
Which Local Dishes to Try?

"食在中国,味在四川",成都作为四川的省会城市,拥有品种丰富的特色川菜可供食客选择。辣和麻是四川菜系最鲜明的味觉特征,但味道多变的川菜还享有"一菜一格,百菜百味"的美誉。四川菜中也有许多不辣的菜品和令人沉醉的美味小吃,火锅在成都永远是不容错过的调动味觉交响的美食风景。

- **特色小吃**

    蒸煮类：叶儿粑、汤圆、三大炮、凉粉

    煎炸类：红糖糍粑、油糕、锅盔、蛋烘糕、糖油果子

    羹汤类：醪糟汤圆、豆花、冰粉

    面食类：担担面、甜水面、杂酱面、水饺、抄手

- **经典菜肴**

    凉　菜：夫妻肺片、蒜泥白肉、红油兔丁、凉拌三丝、各类卤菜

    热　菜：麻婆豆腐、回锅肉、宫保鸡丁、鱼香肉丝、粉蒸肉、蹄花

    其　他：串串香、钵钵鸡、冒菜

- **美食聚集地**

    夜　市：春熙路夜市、抚琴夜市、鹭洲里夜市、大源夜市、玉林夜市、三色路夜市

    美食街：祥和里、香香巷、海椒市、建设路、奎星楼街

"China is the hub for food, and Sichuan is the paradise of flavor." Chengdu has a variety of delicious Sichuan dishes. Spicy and numbing flavors are the most distinctive taste features here, but Sichuan cuisine also enjoys the reputation of "one dish having one style, and one hundred dishes having one hundred flavors." There are also many non-spicy dishes and intoxicating snacks in Sichuan cuisine. Hot pot is always an unmissable food landscape that stimulates taste buds in Chengdu.

• **Unique snacks**
Steamed or boiled snacks: Ye'erba (leaf-wrapped sticky rice dumpling), Tangyuan (sweet dumplings), Sandapao (sticky rice ball), and Liangfen (mung bean jelly noodles)

Pan-fried or deep-fried snacks: Ciba (sticky rice cake with brown sugar sauce), Yougao (fried cake), Guokui (flour pancake), Danhonggao (baked egg cake), and Tangyouguozi (deep-fried glutinous rice ball)

Soupy snacks: Laozaotangyuan (sticky rice balls with fermented sticky rice), Douhua (tofu pudding), and Bingfen (ice jelly)

Noodles and dumplings: Dandanmian (noodles served with spicy sauce), Tianshuimian (sweet thick noodles of Sichuan flavor), Zajiangmian (noodles with bean paste and pork), dumplings, and wontons

- **Classic dishes**

Cold dishes: Fuqifeipian (sliced beef and ox organs in chili sauce), Suannibairou (pork slices with minced garlic), Hongyoutuding (rabbit cubes in red chili oil), Liangbansansi (spicy cold vegetable shreds), and various kinds of braised foods

Hot dishes: Mapo Tofu, Huiguorou (twice-cooked pork), Kung Pao Chicken, Yuxiangrousi (fish-flavored shredded pork), Fenzhengrou (steamed pork with rice flour), and Tihua (pig's trotters)

Others: Chuanchuanxiang (hot pot skewers), Boboji (spicy cold skewers featuring chicken), and Maocai (fast-food hot pot)

- **Where to eat**

Night markets: Chunxi Road Night Market, Fuqin Night Market, Luzhouli Night Market, Dayuan Night Market, Yulin Night Market, and Sanse Road Night Market

Gourmet streets: Xianghe Lane, Xiangxiang Alley, Haijiaoshi Street, Jianshe Road, and Kuixinglou Street

15 / 住宿
Accommodations

基本句 | Basic Sentences

71 wǒ yù dìng le liǎng gè fáng jiān
我 预 订 了 两 个 房 间。
I booked two rooms.

72 kě yǐ huàn gè fáng jiān ma
可 以 换 个 房 间 吗?
Can I switch to a different room?

73 nǐ zhù jǐ lóu
你 住 几 楼?
Which floor are you on?

74 má fan sòng dào hào
麻 烦 送 到 308 号。
Please send it to 308.

75 wǒ yào tuì fáng
我 要 退 房。
I would like to check out.

成都方言 | Chengdu Dialect

ka^1 ka^1 go^2 go^2
旮 旮 角 角：角落
corners

za^2 go^2
咋 个：怎么了
what's going on

$xiao^3$ de^2
晓 得：知道
I know

$ngai^1$ $nong^3$
挨 拢：靠近、挨着
close to; right next to

pu^1 gai^4
铺 盖：被子
quilt

gan^4 sa^4 zi^3
干 啥 子：干什么
what are you doing

住宿怎么选？
How to Choose Accommodations?

成都有众多特色突出的精品酒店和民宿客栈可供选择，以满足商务、旅行需求。从顶级酒店的奢侈享受到民宿客栈的精致实惠，身处温暖湿润的气候之中，仅一处独享的花园露台或一张家居庭院竹制座椅，你就能轻易捕捉到属于成都生活品味中的那份优雅从容、悠闲舒适。

· **根据地理位置选择**

位于公共交通沿线、景点周边的各类酒店和民宿客栈分布相对集中,可根据出行的方便和游玩的线路进行选择。

· **根据住宿偏好选择**

新中式、欧式、轻奢、简约……成都能满足你对各种住宿风格的偏好。如果你有对附带设施(如温泉、泳池、健身房、厨房等)的需求,记得提前咨询。

喜欢热闹繁华,可选择在市中心或各类商圈附近住宿;如果更爱悠闲静谧,建议选择靠近公园、湿地或远离商圈的住宿。

Chengdu has many distinctive boutique hotels and homestay inns that cater to business, travel, and independent tour needs. From the luxury of top hotels to the affordability of homestay inns, in the warm and humid climate, with a garden terrace or a bamboo chair in a home courtyard, one can easily capture the leisure and comfort of Chengdu's lifestyle.

• **Choose according to locations**
Hotels and homestay inns are relatively densely distributed along public transportation routes and around scenic spots. You can choose based on travel convenience and your route planning.

• **Choose according to accommodation preferences**
Chengdu can meet various accommodation style preferences, such as the new Chinese style, the European style, the affordable-luxury style, and the concise style. Remember to consult in advance if you have any demands for accompanying facilities (like hot springs, swimming pools, gyms, kitchens, etc.).

If you like lively and bustling areas, you can choose to stay in the city center or near various commercial districts. If you prefer a more leisurely and peaceful atmosphere, it is recommended to choose places near parks and wetlands, or far from commercial areas.

16 / 游览
Touring

基本句 | Basic Sentences

76 chéng dū yǒu nǎ xiē hǎo wán de dì fang
成都有哪些好玩的地方？
What are some fun places to visit in Chengdu?

77 dà xióng māo zhēn kě ài
大熊猫真可爱！
The giant pandas are adorable!

78 nà shì shén me
那是什么？
What's that?

79 wǒ xiǎng qù kàn biàn liǎn nǐ ne
我想去看变脸，你呢？
I'd like to watch a *bianlian* (face changing) show. How about you?

80 nǐ néng bāng wǒ pāi zhāng zhào piàn ma
你能帮我拍张照片吗？
Could you please take a picture for me?

成都方言 | Chengdu Dialect

xiong² qi³
雄 起：加油、助威
come on (to show encouragement and support)

kai¹ qiang¹
开 腔：说话
to speak

dui⁴ tou²
对 头：应答语，表示肯定、正确
a response to express affirmation

o³ ho⁴
哦 嗬：语气词，指糟糕了，表示感叹、惋惜或无奈
an exclamation for something bad, or to sigh, or to express regret or helplessness

bai³ nong² men² zen⁴
摆 龙 门 阵：聊天，讲故事
to chat and tell stories

特色景点在哪里?
Where to Visit?

　　作为文化休闲名城、古蜀文明发祥地,成都不仅有令人向往的历史古迹和可爱的熊猫,还有绚丽的都市景观和迷人的自然风光。城市周边有中国一流的人文自然景区和古镇。徜徉在包容而好客的成都,会感叹这真是一座能让人梦想成真的美好城市。

- **历史古迹**

    宽窄巷子、武侯祠、锦里、杜甫草堂

- **公园及游乐场**

    熊猫基地、人民公园、望江楼公园、浣花溪公园、三圣乡、欢乐谷

- **商业街区及创意产业基地**

    太古里、春熙路、铁像寺水街、东郊记忆、U37创意仓库、望平街

- **博物馆及展览馆**

    四川博物院、成都博物馆、四川科技馆、三星堆博物馆、金沙遗址博物馆、川菜博物馆

- **成都周边游**

    都江堰、青城山、黄龙溪古镇、街子古镇、平乐古镇、安仁古镇、洛带古镇

As a city of cultural and leisure activities, and the birthplace of ancient Shu civilization, Chengdu has not only fascinating historical sites and lovely giant pandas, but also splendid urban landscapes and mesmerizing natural scenery. The city is surrounded by top-tier cultural and natural scenic areas and ancient towns. Wandering in the inclusive and hospitable Chengdu, one would feel that it is truly a dream city that makes people's dreams come true.

• Historical sites
Kuan Zhai Xiangzi (wide and narrow alleys), Wuhou Shrine, Jinli Ancient Street, and the Thatched Cottage of Du Fu

• Parks and amusement parks
Chengdu Research Base of Giant Panda Breeding, People's Park, Wangjianglou Park, Huanhuaxi Park, Sansheng Township, and Happy Valley

• Business streets and creative industry bases
Taikoo Li, Chunxi Road, Tiexiang Temple Riverfront, Eastern Suburb Memory, U37 Loft, and Wangping Street

• **Museums and exhibition halls**
Sichuan Museum, Chengdu Museum, Sichuan Science and Technology Museum, Sanxingdui Museum, Jinsha Site Museum, and Sichuan Cuisine Museum

• **Destinations around Chengdu**
Dujiangyan (the Dujiangyan Irrigation System), Qingcheng Mountian, Huanglongxi Ancient Town, Jiezi Ancient Town, Pingle Ancient Town, Anren Ancient Town, and Luodai Ancient Town

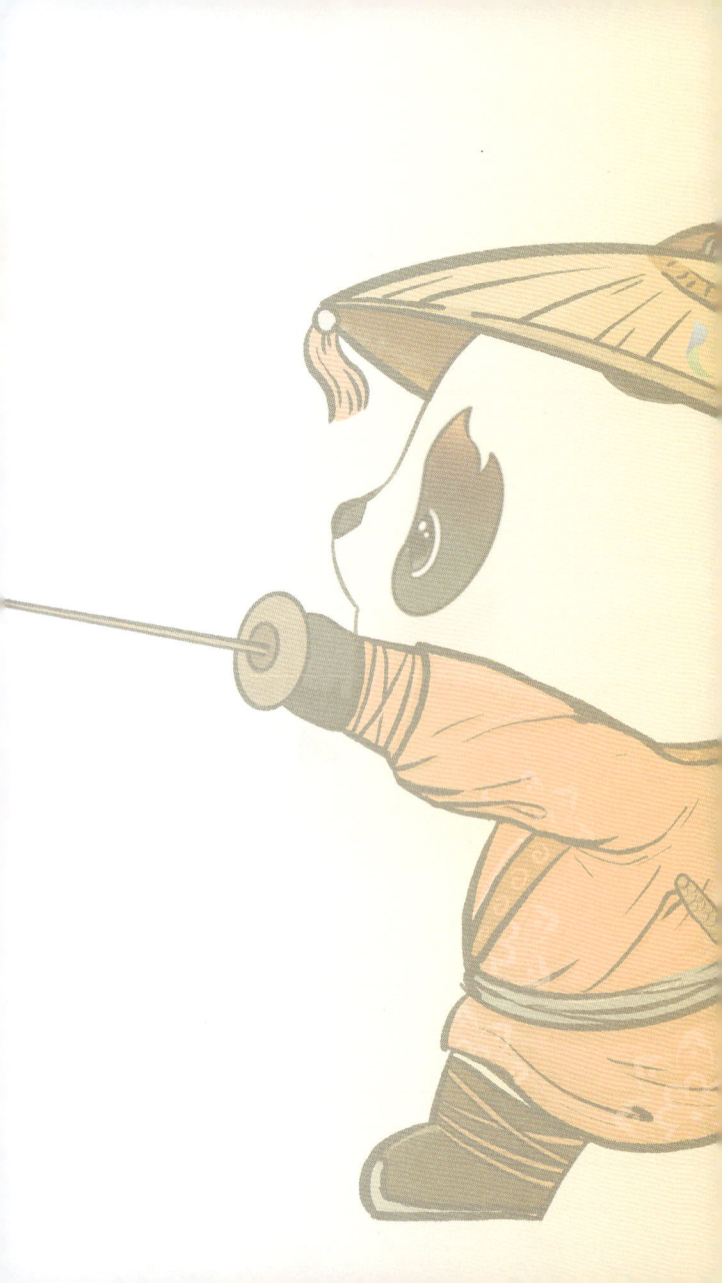

17 / 购物
Shopping

基本句 | Basic Sentences

81 yí gòng duō shao qián
一共多少钱？
How much in total?

82 wǒ xiǎng mǎi xiē sì chuān tè chǎn
我想买些四川特产。
I want to buy some Sichuan specialties.

83 wǒ méi yǒu xiàn jīn kě yǐ shuā kǎ ma
我没有现金，可以刷卡吗？
I don't have any cash. Can I pay by credit/debit card?

84 hái yǒu qí tā yán sè ma
还有其他颜色吗？
Are other colors available?

85 wǒ yào sān bāo huǒ guō dǐ liào wǔ gè jí xiáng wù
我要三包火锅底料，五个吉祥物。
I would like three bags of hot pot soup base, and five mascots.

成都方言 | Chengdu Dialect

yang² pan²
洋 盘：时髦
trendy

xiang¹ yin¹
相 因：便宜
cheap

zou² bu² to²
走 不 脱：形容无法脱身的状态
to be stuck in a troublesome situation

an⁴
咹：感叹词，答应时表示疑惑、疑问
an exclamation to express doubt or confusion when used as a response

购物逛街买什么?
What to Buy?

市井街巷深处的慢生活与时尚都市的繁华,使得成都能满足古老与现代交织的多元而丰富的购物需求。

· **成都特产**

火锅底料、辣椒油、辣椒粉、郫县豆瓣、灯影牛肉、宫廷糕点、老妈兔头、川茶、川酒、熊猫周边产品

· **重要商圈**

城中心:春熙路-盐市口商圈等

城　南:交子商圈、大源商圈等

城　东:建设路商圈等

城　北:蓉北商圈等

城　西:金沙光华商圈、武侯双楠商圈等

An appealing combination of tradition and modernity, Chengdu affords a diversified range of shopping options.

• **Chengdu specialties**
hot pot soup base, chili oil, chili powder, Pixian thick broad-bean sauce, Dengying Beef (film-thin beef slices), Gongting Pastry, Laoma (Old Mom) Rabbit Head, Sichuan tea, Sichuan liquor, and giant panda-themed products

• **Important business circles**
Downtown area: Chunxi Road-Yanshikou business circle, among others
South of the city: Jiaozi business circle, Dayuan business circle, etc.
East of the city: Jianshe Road business circle, among others
North of the city: Rongbei business circle, among others
West of the city: Jinsha Guanghua business circle, Wuhou Shuangnan business circle, etc.

18 / 邀请
Invitations

基本句 | Basic Sentences

86 míng tiān wǎn shang yǒu shí jiān ma
明 天 晚 上 有 时 间 吗?
Do you have time tomorrow night?

87 hē kā fēi ma wǒ qǐng kè
喝 咖 啡 吗? 我 请 客。
Want some coffee? It's on me!

88 nǐ néng hé wǒ yì qǐ qù kàn diàn yǐng ma
你 能 和 我 一 起 去 看 电 影 吗?
Could you go with me for a movie?

89 yì yán wéi dìng bú jiàn bú sàn
一 言 为 定,不 见 不 散。
See you there. I'll wait till you show up.

90 huān yíng nǐ lái dào wǒ men de guó jiā
欢 迎 你 来 到 我 们 的 国 家。
Welcome to our country.

词汇拓展 | Vocabulary Extension

tài yáng xì
太 阳 系
the solar system

yín hé xì
银 河 系
the Galaxy

kē huàn piàn
科 幻 片
sci-fi film

dì qiú
地 球
the Earth

值得了解的中国科幻文化
Insights into China's Sci-Fi Culture

在中国，科幻爱好者是一个较大的文化群体，科幻类型的影视很受年轻人欢迎。《流浪地球》是中国第一部硬科幻电影，展现了中国电影人对"宇宙"这一宏大命题的探索，该片获得第32届中国电影金鸡奖最佳故事片奖。

《三体》是科幻作家刘慈欣声誉极高的一部巨作，书中关于科技与文明关系的深刻思考，受到很多读者的肯定，电视剧和动画片同样赢得广大科幻迷的认同。

科幻文化及其影视产业在中国的发展，给中国乃至世界拓宽了独具特色的科学想象空间。2023年10月即将在成都举办的第81届世界科幻大会，将以"共生纪元"为主题，邀请全世界的朋友共话科幻未来。

In China, sci-fi fans form a large cultural group, and sci-fi films and TV shows are popular among young people. As China's first hard sci-fi film, *The Wandering Earth* reflects the exploration of the grand theme, the universe, by the filmmaking community in the country. It won the best feature award at the 32nd Golden Rooster Awards in 2019.

The Three-Body Problem trilogy is a highly acclaimed masterpiece by Chinese sci-fi writer Liu Cixin. It has been widely recognized by many readers for its profound thinking on the relationship between technology and civilization. The TV series and animated adaptation have also drawn accolades from sci-fi fans.

The development of sci-fi culture and the film and television industry in China has offered the country and the world a unique space for scientific imagination. The 81st World Science Fiction Convention to be held in Chengdu in October 2023, with Coexistence Era as its theme, will invite friends from all over the world to talk about the future of science fiction.

19 / 聚会
Participating in Gatherings

基本句 | Basic Sentences

91 gān bēi
干 杯!
Cheers!

92 gǎn xiè nǐ de chū xí
感 谢 你 的 出 席。
Thank you for your attendance.

93 fēi cháng róng xìng
非 常 荣 幸!
My pleasure!

94 zhè shì wǒ zài sān xīng duī bó wù guǎn gěi nǐ mǎi de lǐ wù
这 是 我 在 三 星 堆 博 物 馆 给 你 买 的 礼 物。
This is a gift for you. I bought this in the Sanxingdui Museum.

95 zhù dà yùn huì yuán mǎn chéng gōng
祝 大 运 会 圆 满 成 功!
Wish a complete success for the Chengdu 2021 FISU Games!

词汇拓展 | Vocabulary Extension

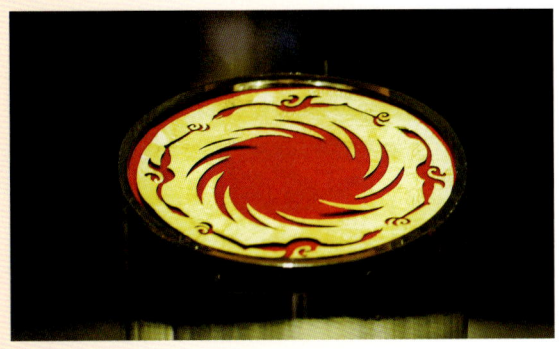

tài yáng shén niǎo
太 阳 神 鸟
Golden Sun Bird

qín shǐ huáng bīng mǎ yǒng
秦 始 皇 兵 马 俑
Terracotta Army of Qin Shihuang (First Emperor of Qin)

zēng hóu yǐ biān zhōng
曾 侯 乙 编 钟
Bianzhong (bronze bells) of Marquis Yi of the State of Zeng

hòu mǔ wù dǐng
后 母 戊 鼎
Houmuwu Ding (three-legged bronze cauldron)

sān cǎi luò tuo zài yuè yǒng
三 彩 骆 驼 载 乐 俑
Tricolor Glazed Pottery Camel Carrying Musicians

考古文化中的年轻精神
Youth Reinvigorates Chinese Archeology

位于四川广汉的三星堆遗址考古新发现——龟背形网格状青铜器——被年轻人戏称为"古代烧烤架",由此引发三星堆"盲盒"上新的话题;位于陕西西安的秦始皇帝陵博物院(秦始皇兵马俑博物馆)首次公布修复完成的"仰卧俑",因为形态很像在做仰卧起坐而备受网友瞩目;沉没150多年的古商船"长江口二号"被成功整体打捞出水,激发起年轻人对水下考古的兴趣和对位于上海的中国航海博物馆的关注……

古老的文明、神秘的历史未解之谜和中国当代年轻人之间,就这样一次又一次地进行着跨越时空的有趣交流,希望你也能感受到这年轻而富有活力的气息,感受到和这里的每一种文化邂逅时的轻松和快乐。

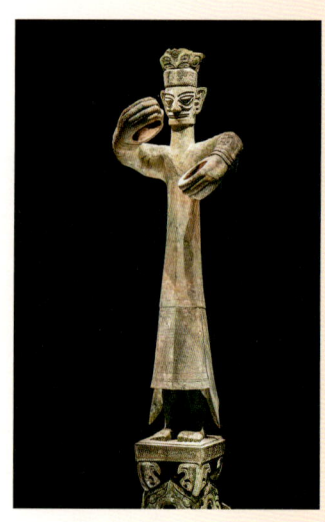

The bronze vessel covered with tortoise-shaped reticulate lids newly discovered at the Sanxingdui Ruins site in Guanghan, Sichuan, is jokingly named "ancient BBQ grill" by young people, which has triggered new discussions on Sanxingdui-themed blind box products. The restored supine figure from the Emperor Qinshihuang's Mausoleum Site Museum (Terracotta Army Museum) in Xi'an, Shaanxi, has attracted wide attention on Chinese social media platforms because of its distinctive gesture which bears high similarity to doing sit-ups. The Yangtze River Estuary No. 2, an ancient merchant ship salvaged as a whole more than 150 years after it sank, has aroused young people's interest in underwater archeology and the China Maritime Museum in Shanghai. And the list goes on.

Ancient civilization, historical mysteries, and China's new generation are communicating in interesting ways. Hopefully, you can also feel the youthful atmosphere and enjoy your encounter with every culture here.

20 / 祝福
Expressing Good Wishes

基本句 | Basic Sentences

96 wǒ ài nǐ men
我 爱 你 们！
I love you all!

97 zhù nǐ yí lù píng ān
祝 你 一 路 平 安！
Have a safe trip!

98 xī wàng yǐ hòu hái néng xiāng jù
希 望 以 后 还 能 相 聚！
Hope to see you again sometime!

99 zhōng guó gěi wǒ liú xià le měi hǎo de yìn xiàng
中 国 给 我 留 下 了 美 好 的 印 象。
China has left a wonderful impression on me.

100 wǒ yí dìng huì zài lái
我 一 定 会 再 来！
I will definitely come back!

词汇拓展 | Vocabulary Extension

wài mài
外卖
food delivery service

gāo tiě
高铁
high-speed railway

wǎng gòu
网购
online shopping

lǜ dào
绿道
greenway

sǎo mǎ zhī fù
扫码支付
scan a QR code to pay

quán mín jiàn shēn
全民健身
national fitness

中国的数字生活新方式
The New Digital Lifestyle in China

当你来到中国,会发现数字生活方式已经渗透到中国人日常生活的每一个角落。从衣食住行到娱乐消费,数字技术为智慧生活提供着各种便利。

当人们出行时,无论开车、骑行还是步行,都在使用手机里的导航软件,导航软件还会将目的地周边的美食、商店、住宿、医院等信息,智能地推荐给使用者。物流的高效使得购物软件的应用在中国极为普遍,人们通过电商平台购买服装、食品等生活用品,甚至可以购买新鲜水果和蔬菜。

移动支付、数码点餐、健身运动、线上就医、数字教育、电子政务……除此之外,智慧停车、垃圾智能分类回收等不断涌现的数字应用新场景,还在刷新着中国数字生活方式的新纪录。中国的数字生活新方式同时也给人们带来了新习惯、新文化和新业态。

When you come to China, you will find that the digital lifestyle has penetrated into every corner of people's daily lives. From clothing, food, housing, and transportation to entertainment, digital technologies have brought a variety of conveniences for smart living.

When people travel, whether by car, bicycle, or on foot, they use navigation apps on their mobile phones. The apps also intelligently recommend information about food, shops, accommodations, hospitals, and other places around the destination to the user. Efficient logistics make shopping apps very popular in China. People buy daily necessities such as clothing and food, and even fresh fruits and vegetables through e-commerce platforms.

Mobile payment, digital ordering, digital fitness, online medical services, digital education, e-government services, just to name a few. And innovations based on digital technologies such as smart parking and intelligent waste classification and recycling are bringing new upgrades to people's digital lifestyle. The digital transformation has also given rise to new habits, new cultures, and new business models in China.

成都，
成就梦想！

Chengdu Makes Dreams Come True!

朋友，
欢迎你们！

Welcome, my friends!

  本书图片来自成都第 31 届世界大学生夏季运动会执委会、四川画报社等,蓉宝创作来自田海稣教授。谨向所有为本书提供帮助的机构、单位及人士致以诚挚的谢意!

  本书附有数字资源,可扫描封底二维码阅览电子书,并根据音频学说大运中文 100 句。

We would like to thank the Executive Committee of the Chengdu 2021 FISU World University Games and Sichuan Pictorial Press, among others, for permission to reproduce photographs. A debt is owed to Prof. Tian Haisu for her creating the cute images of Rongbao. Our sincere gratitude is extended to all that have provided assistance during the preparation of this book.

You can scan the QR code on the back cover to read the e-version of this book, and access the audio resources to learn the 100 Chinese sentences for the Chengdu 2021 FISU World University Games.

图书在版编目(CIP)数据

大运中文100句:汉文、英文 / 中外语言交流合作中心组编. -- 成都:四川人民出版社,2023.7
ISBN 978-7-220-13311-4

Ⅰ.①大… Ⅱ.①中… Ⅲ.①世界大学生运动会—汉语—对外汉语教学—自学参考资料—汉、英 Ⅳ.①H195.4

中国国家版本馆CIP数据核字(2023)第114644号

DAYUN ZHONGWEN 100 JU
大运中文100句

中外语言交流合作中心 组编

出版人	黄立新
责任编辑	秦 莉 范雯晴
英文审校	柳 畔
封面绘制	田海鲦
装帧设计	张迪茗
责任校对	舒晓利 申婷婷
责任印制	周 奇
出版发行	四川人民出版社(成都市三色路238号)
网 址	http://www.scpph.com
E-mail	scrmcbs@sina.com
新浪微博	@四川人民出版社
微信公众号	四川人民出版社
发行部业务电话	(028)86361653 86361656
防盗版举报电话	(028)86361653
照 排	四川胜翔数码印务设计有限公司
印 刷	四川新财印务有限公司
成品尺寸	105mm×170mm
印 张	4.875
字 数	97千
版 次	2023年7月第1版
印 次	2023年7月第1次印刷
书 号	ISBN 978-7-220-13311-4
定 价	45.00元

■版权所有·侵权必究

本书若出现印装质量问题,请与我社发行部联系调换
电话:(028)86361656